Frank Schaffer Publications®

S0-APO-413

Published by Ideal School Supply
An imprint of Frank Schaffer Publications
Copyright © 1999 School Specialty Publishing
All Rights Reserved • Printed in China

Send all inquiries to:
Frank Schaffer Publications
8720 Orion Place
Columbus, OH 43240
Flip-Flash™ Math: Multiplication & Division Facts

10 11 12 13 WKT 10 09 08

Helpful Hints for Learning the Facts

Flip and Check Say the answer to a fact, then flip the page to check.
The answer is the first number on the flip side of the page.

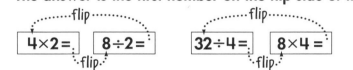

Double Your Power Learn the double-number facts.
Use them to help you remember other facts.

| $3 \times 3 =$ | $5 \times 5 =$ | $10 \times 10 =$ |

Power Up With Turnarounds Learn pairs of "turnaround" facts.
If you know one, you know the other one too.

| $2 \times 9 =$ | $9 \times 2 =$ | $6 \times 9 =$ | $9 \times 6 =$ |

Tackle the Hard Ones
Find the facts that give you trouble.
Draw a picture to help you "see"
the fact in your mind.

$6 \times 7 =$

$$\begin{array}{ccccccc} \times & \times & \times & \times & \times & \times & \times \\ \times & \times & \times & \times & \times & \times & \times \\ \times & \times & \times & \times & \times & \times & \times \\ \times & \times & \times & \times & \times & \times & \times \\ \times & \times & \times & \times & \times & \times & \times \\ \times & \times & \times & \times & \times & \times & \times \end{array}$$

Make It a Game Make up games to help you recall
the facts quickly. Play the games with your friends and family.

Multiplication Chart

X	1	2	3	4	5	6	7	8	9	10	11	12
1	1	2	3	4	5	6	7	8	9	10	11	12
2	2	4	6	8	10	12	14	16	18	20	22	24
3	3	6	9	12	15	18	21	24	27	30	33	36
4	4	8	12	16	20	24	28	32	36	40	44	48
5	5	10	15	20	25	30	35	40	45	50	55	60
6	6	12	18	24	30	36	42	48	54	60	66	72
7	7	14	21	28	35	42	49	56	63	70	77	84
8	8	16	24	32	40	48	56	64	72	80	88	96
9	9	18	27	36	45	54	63	72	81	90	99	108
10	10	20	30	40	50	60	70	80	90	100	110	120
11	11	22	33	44	55	66	77	88	99	110	121	132
12	12	24	36	48	60	72	84	96	108	120	132	144

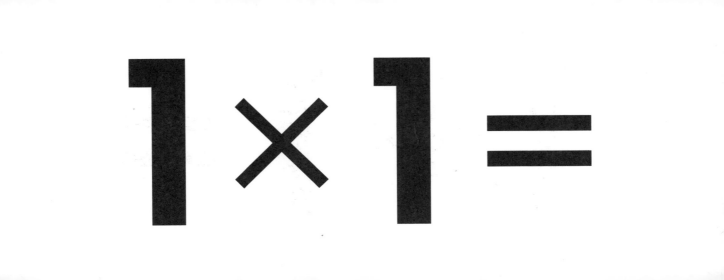

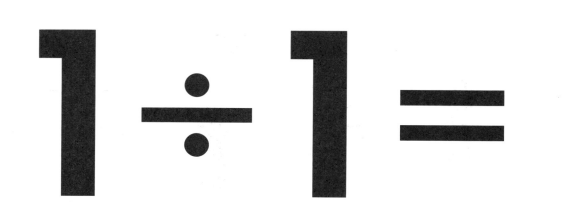

$$1 \times 2 =$$

$$2 \div 2 =$$

1 × 4 =

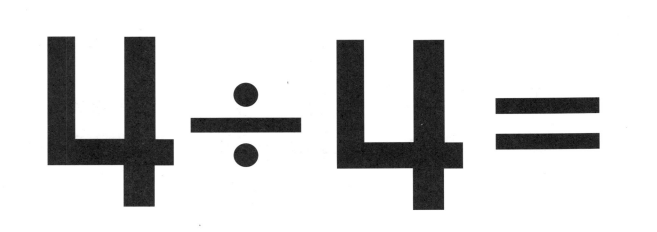

$$1 \times 6 =$$

$$6 \div 6 =$$

$$1 \times 8 =$$

$$8 \div 8 =$$

$$1 \times 10 =$$

10 ÷ 10 =

1 × 12 =

12÷12=

$$2 \times 2 =$$

$$4 \div 2 =$$

$$2 \times 3 =$$

$$6 \div 3 =$$

$$2 \times 5 =$$

$$10 \div 5 =$$

$2 \times 7 =$

$$14 \div 7 =$$

$$2 \times 9 =$$

$$18 \div 9 =$$

2×11=

22÷11=

3×1=

$$3 \div 1 =$$

$$3 \times 3 =$$

$$9 \div 3 =$$

$$3 \times 4 =$$

$$12 \div 4 =$$

$$3 \times 6 =$$

$$18 \div 6 =$$

$$3 \times 8 =$$

$$24 \div 8 =$$

$3 \times 10 =$

$$30 \div 10 =$$

$$3 \times 12 =$$

$$36 \div 12 =$$

$$4 \times 2 =$$

$$8 \div 2 =$$

4 × 4 =

16 ÷ 4 =

4 × 5 =

$$20 \div 5 =$$

$$4 \times 7 =$$

$$28 \div 7 =$$

$4 \times 9 =$

$$36 \div 9 =$$

4×11=

44÷11=

$5 \times 1 =$

$$5 \div 1 =$$

5 × 3 =

15 ÷ 3 =

$$5 \times 5 =$$

$$25 \div 5 =$$

$5 \times 6 =$

$$30 \div 6 =$$

$$5 \times 8 =$$

$$40 \div 8 =$$

5 × 10 =

50 ÷ 10 =

5 × 12 =

$$60 \div 12 =$$

6 × 2 =

$$12 \div 2 =$$

$6 \times 4 =$

$$24 \div 4 =$$

$$6 \times 6 =$$

$$36 \div 6 =$$

$6 \times 7 =$

$$42 \div 7 =$$

$$6 \times 9 =$$

$$54 \div 9 =$$

$6 \times 11 =$

$$66 \div 11 =$$

7 × 1 =

$$7 \div 1 =$$

$$7 \times 3 =$$

$$21 \div 3 =$$

$$7 \times 5 =$$

$$35 \div 5 =$$

$$7 \times 7 =$$

49 ÷ 7 =

$$7 \times 8 =$$

$$56 \div 8 =$$

$$7 \times 10 =$$

70 ÷ 10 =

$$7 \times 12 =$$

$$84 \div 12 =$$

16 ÷ 2 =

$8 \times 4 =$

$$32 \div 4 =$$

$$8 \times 6 =$$

48 ÷ 6 =

64÷8=

$$8 \times 9 =$$

72 ÷ 9 =

88 ÷ 11 =

9×1=

9 ÷ 1 =

$$9 \times 3 =$$

$$27 \div 3 =$$

$9 \times 5 =$

45÷5=

9 × 7 =

63 ÷ 7 =

9 × 9 =

81 ÷ 9 =

$$9 \times 10 =$$

90 ÷ 10 =

9×12=

108÷12=

10×2=

$$20 \div 2 =$$

$$10 \times 4 =$$

40 ÷ 4 =

10 × 6 =

60 ÷ 6 =

$$10 \times 8 =$$

$$80 \div 8 =$$

10×10 =

$$100 \div 10 =$$

10×11=

110÷11=

$$11 \div 1 =$$

$$11 \times 3 =$$

$$33 \div 3 =$$

$$11 \times 5 =$$

$$55 \div 5 =$$

$11 \times 7 =$

$$77 \div 7 =$$

11 × 9 =

99 ÷ 9 =

121÷11=

11×12=

132÷12=

12×2=

$$24 \div 2 =$$

12×4=

48 ÷ 4 =

12×6=

72 ÷ 6 =

12×8=

$$96 \div 8 =$$

12×10 =

120÷10=

12×12=

144÷12=